Before They Were Famous

Thomas Edison

Written by Stephen Krensky
Illustrated by Bobbie Houser

A Crabtree Crown Book

CRABTREE
Publishing Company
www.crabtreebooks.com

School-to-Home Support for Caregivers and Teachers

This appealing book is designed to teach students about core subject areas. Students will build upon what they already know about the subject, and engage in topics that they want to learn more about. Here are a few guiding questions to help readers build their comprehension skills. Possible answers appear here in red.

Before Reading:

What do I know about this topic?

- I know that Thomas Edison was a great inventor, and that he invented the light bulb.
- I know that the phonograph was also invented by Thomas Edison.

What do I want to learn about this topic?

- I want to learn more about the many inventions of Thomas Edison.
- I want to learn more about the time period when Thomas Edison lived.

During Reading:

I'm curious to know...

- I'm curious to know what types of books Edison liked to read.
- I wonder if any of Thomas Edison's invention blew up or caught fire.

How is this like something I already know?

- I have read about experiments going wrong, exploding, and damaging buildings.
- When someone saves the life of a child it's not unusual for the parents to want to give something of value to the hero. Knowledge of Morse code was the gift given to Thomas.

After Reading:

What was the author trying to teach me?

- I think the author is trying to teach the fact that if you want to achieve great things you must persevere, work hard, and never give up on your dreams.
- I think the author wanted to teach people that no matter how different some people may appear, they may be capable of great things.

How did the photographs and captions help me understand more?

- The photographs showed me the types of clothing worn during Thomas Edison's life.
- I enjoyed reading the captions and learning more about Morse code and how it replaced the Pony Express.

Table of Contents

Train Rides

Thomas Edison was very happy. He was only 12 years old, and already he was running his own business.

ALL ABOARD!

And this business was always on the move. Why? Because it was based on a train that ran 100 miles (160 kilometers) from Port Huron, Michigan to Detroit, Michigan.

Fun Facts

Alva, shortened to Al, was Thomas Edison's middle name.

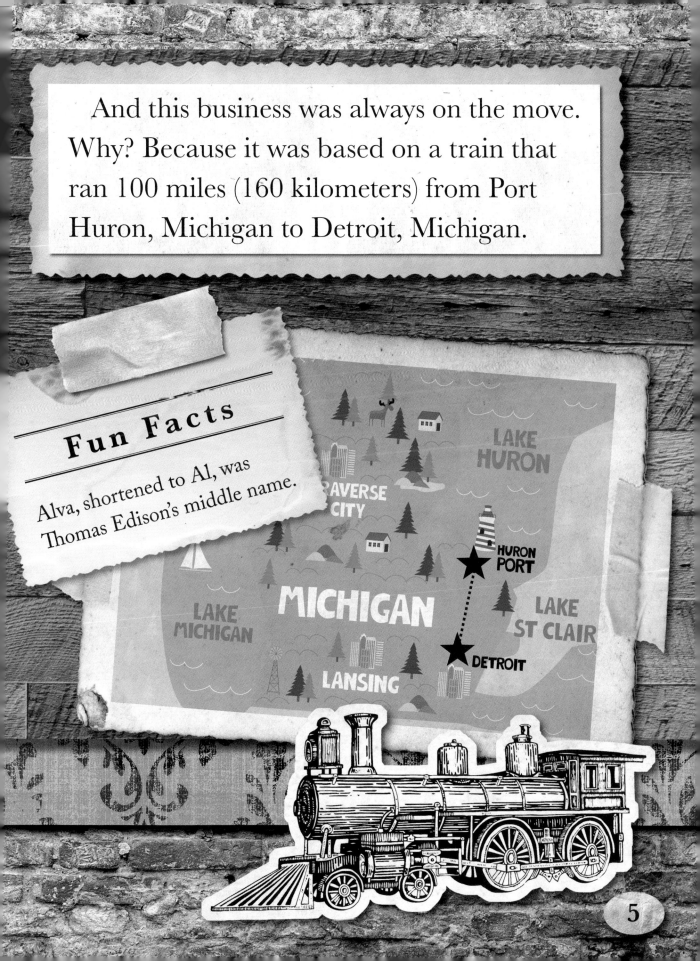

Al, as Thomas was known, was a familiar face to the train passengers. He rode the train most days, earning money by selling candy and vegetables.

Samuel Edison

Nancy Edison

Thomas Edison, age 3

Family Tree

Later, he also sold the *Grand Trunk Herald*, a newspaper he wrote and printed about the news of the day. The news itself he copied from information sent to station offices along the train route.

An Unusual Education

Al had plenty of time to spend on the train because he wasn't in school. Actually, he had only gone there for a few months when he was younger. Al was curious and imaginative, but he found it difficult to sit still and pay attention at school.

Fun Facts

Al had a harder time at school because he was partially deaf. He had been sick with several ear infections and **scarlet fever**.

His teacher had trouble dealing with him. She said he was unable to focus on his studies and easily distracted.

Al's mother didn't agree with the teacher. And that meant something, since Nancy Edison was a former schoolteacher herself. Al wasn't easy, she knew that, but not easy didn't mean he couldn't learn. So she taught Al reading, writing, and arithmetic at home. He learned a lot of other things, though, just by reading on his own.

BOOKS

Fun Facts

Before he was done, Al had read every book in his local library.

Al was **fascinated** by science. Most of the **profits** from his job on the train went to buy electrical and chemical supplies. Then he spent long hours using them to do different experiments.

Michael Faraday

Fun Facts

Al was inspired by the work of Michael Faraday, an English scientist whose ideas led to the creation of the electric generator in 1831.

Al even got permission to conduct some experiments in a small **laboratory** he set up in the train's baggage car. That was not a problem until one day when some of his chemicals caught fire and started burning the train car.

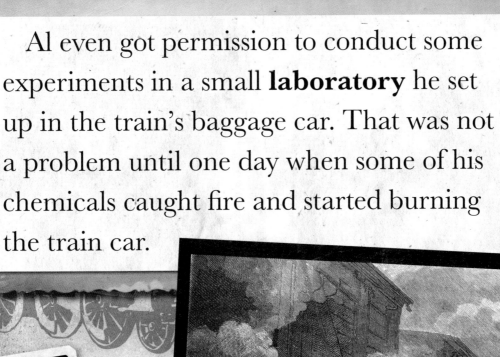

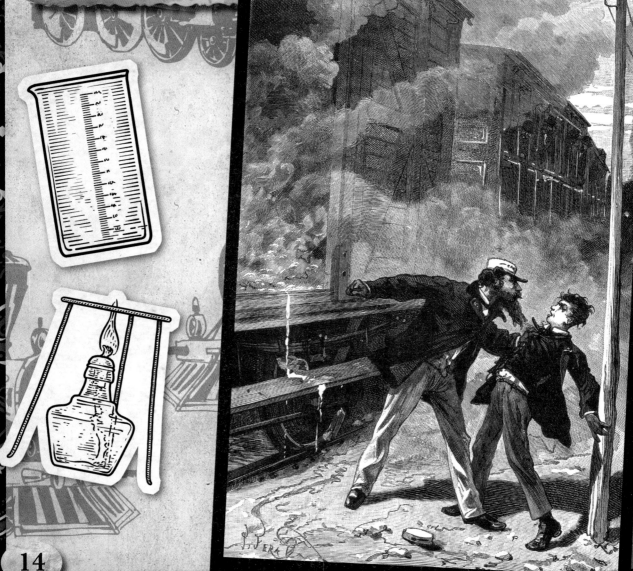

Nobody was hurt, but after that Al did his future experimenting on solid ground.

Fun Facts

Al's first laboratory was set up in his parents' basement when he was ten years old.

A Key Moment

Everyone who worked around the train stations knew Al, and over time he made some new friends. One of them was James Mackenzie, a **stationmaster** and **telegraph** officer.

Al also got to know Mr. Mackenzie's two-year-old son Jimmie, who often played nearby while his father worked.

PRESSURE GAUGE

Fun Facts

The average speed on most trains at the time was only about 20 miles (32 km) an hour.

Trains were always coming and going near the station. One summer day, 15-year-old Al noticed little Jimmie playing on one of the tracks.

Most of the time that might be perfectly safe. But not that day. A **boxcar** was rolling toward them, and Jimmie was right in its way.

Thomas Edison, age 15

Fun Facts

Boxcars were made of wood until the late 1800s, when they began to be made of steel.

Luckily, Al saw what was happening. There was not a moment to spare. Ignoring any risk to himself, Al jumped down onto the tracks, grabbed Jimmie, and leaped to the side just before the boxcar rumbled past.

Jimmie's father found them both a little bumped and bruised. But otherwise they were fine.

Mr. Mackenzie couldn't thank Al enough for saving Jimmie's life. But he wanted to do more than just shake his hand a few times. So he offered to teach Al **Morse code**, the series of dots and dashes that were used to send messages by telegraph.

Fun Facts

Morse code was first used in the late 1830s, a few years after the telegraph was **invented**.

SOS
Save Our Souls

TELEGRAM

Form No.1

No............ | Time Sent.................. | To{
Time Received......................

MORSE CODE

A ● ▬	N ▬ ●			
B ▬ ● ● ●	O ▬ ▬ ▬			
C ▬ ● ▬ ●	P ● ▬ ▬ ●			
D ▬ ● ●	Q ▬ ▬ ● ▬	1 ● ▬ ▬ ▬ ▬		
E ●	R ● ▬ ●	2 ● ● ▬ ▬ ▬		
F ● ● ▬ ●	S ● ● ●	3 ● ● ● ▬ ▬		
G ▬ ▬ ●	T ▬	4 ● ● ● ● ▬		
H ● ● ● ●	U ● ● ▬	5 ● ● ● ● ●		
I ● ●	V ● ● ● ▬	6 ▬ ● ● ● ●		
J ● ▬ ▬ ▬	W ● ▬ ▬	7 ▬ ▬ ● ● ●		
K ▬ ● ▬	X ▬ ● ● ▬	8 ▬ ▬ ▬ ● ●		
L ● ▬ ● ●	Y ▬ ● ▬ ▬	9 ▬ ▬ ▬ ▬ ●		
M ▬ ▬	Z ▬ ▬ ● ●	0 ▬ ▬ ▬ ▬ ▬		

Learning His Craft

Al was thrilled, and he spent all of his free time practicing Morse code. It wasn't just a question of learning which dots and dashes stood for which letters in the alphabet. He also needed to tap out the code fast enough for a message to be sent out quickly and also understand the code fast enough to turn a received message back into words.

Fun Facts

Later, when he had children, Edison nicknamed the first two Dot and Dash.

It turned out that Al was very good at using Morse code. In fact, within a few months he was good enough to get a job as a telegraph operator.

He was young for the job, but the only thing that really mattered was that he could get the job done. And there was no question about that.

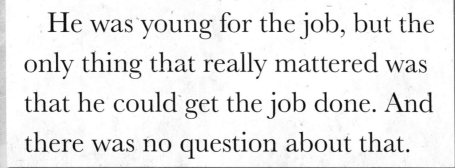

Fun Facts

Before the telegraph system, the Pony Express provided the fastest delivery of messages in the U.S. Riders on horseback galloped from town to town delivering mail and newspapers.

After a few years, Al began traveling through the Midwest, working wherever a telegrapher was needed. At the same time, he learned a lot more about telegraph technology and electrical science in general.

Al rented a room here in Louisville, Kentucky, while working as a telegraph operator.

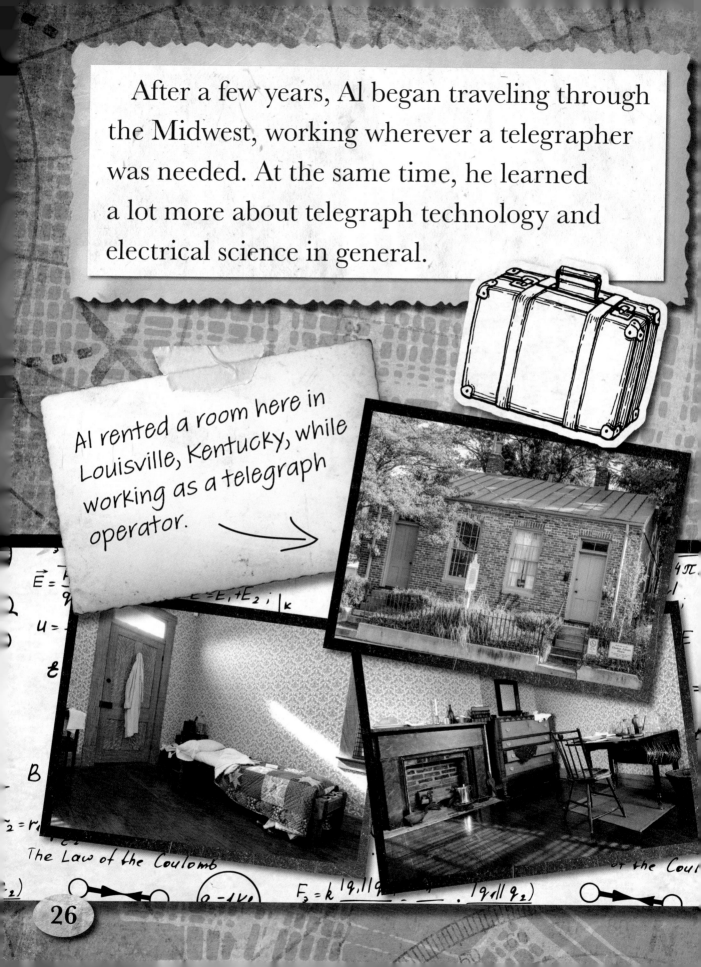

$\vec{E} = $

$u = $

$\mathcal{E}$

$E = E_1 + E_2 ;$

B

$_2 = r$

The Law of the Coulomb

$F_3 = k \frac{|q_1||q_2|}{}$. $|q_1||q_2|)$

the Cou

But he hadn't forgotten about his experiments. Even as he continued working, Al also tried to invent things.

Fun Facts

Edison's first invention was an automatic vote counter, but no one was interested in buying it.

Inventing the Future

At the age of 22, Al moved to New York City and sold his first invention. It was an improved stock ticker that could keep track of company stock sales much faster than existing machines.

For the first time, Al began to wonder if maybe he could make a career out of being an inventor. Was this possible? He had no idea. But he was willing to try and see what would happen next.

Thomas Alva Edison was only 29 years old when he received a **patent** for the incandescent light bulb in 1880, the invention that made him a household name. He had already used the profits from earlier inventions to set up an inventing workshop in Menlo Park, New Jersey.

The Wizard of Menlo Park, as Edison came to be known, received 1,093 patents for all the inventions he created with his staff. Among them were the **phonograph** and the movie camera. Although often called a genius for his output, Edison countered this by saying, "Genius is one percent inspiration and ninety-nine percent perspiration." He also reportedly said, "Opportunity is missed by most people because it is dressed in overalls and looks like work."

Edison died at the age of 84 in 1931.

29

GLOSSARY

boxcar
A train car designed to carry freight with sliding doors on the side

fascinated
Strongly attracted to or interested in

invented
Created something new

laboratory
A room devoted to scientific research

Morse code
A system of dots and dashes, each one representing one letter of the English alphabet

patent
An official document that gives someone the right to be the only one that makes or sells a product for a certain period of time

phonograph
An instrument that reproduces sounds recorded on a grooved disk

profits
The extra money left over after the cost of something being sold is paid for

scarlet fever
A serious illness that causes a red rash, sore throat, and fever

stationmaster
A person in charge of the comings and goings at a train station

telegraph
A device for communicating that uses electricity to send coded messages through wires

INDEX

COMPREHENSION QUESTIONS

How long did Edison go to school?

Whose life did Edison save?

What was the first invention Edison sold?

ABOUT THE AUTHOR

Stephen Krensky is the award-winning author of more than 150 fiction and nonfiction books for children. He and his wife Joan live in Lexington, Massachusetts, and he happily spends as much time as possible with his grown children and not-so-grown grandchildren.

CRABTREE
Publishing Company

Written by: Stephen Krensky

Illustrations by: Bobbie Houser

Art direction and layout by: Bobbie Houser

Series Development: James Earley

Proofreader: Petrice Custance

Educational Consultant: Marie Lemke M.Ed.

Print Coordinator: Katherine Berti

Photographs: t = Top, c = Center, b = Bottom, l = Left, r = Right
Alamy: Smith Archive: pp. 7 tc, tr, 22; Ilene MacDonald: p. 15 tr; Photo Researchers/Science History Images: p. 24 t; Pictures Now: p. 25 tl; World Archive: p. 25 cl; Thomas Kelley: p. 26 cr; Daniel Dempster Photography: p. 26 bl, br; Granger: Sarin Images: p. 6 t; pp. 7 cl, 14. r; Interfoto: p. 18 t; Shutterstock: Rawpixel.com: cover tl; Everett Collection: cover bl, pp. 13 t, 28, 29 b; James Steidl: cover br; Mascha Tace: p. 4; Mio Buono: p. 5 t; Vorobiov Oleksii 8: p. 5 b; bioraven: p. 6 b; Thammanoon Khamchalee: p. 7 cr; shin88: p. 7 c; VladisChern: p. 7 b; fotohay: p. 8 t; Photology1971: p. 8 b; colors: p. 9; Redshinestudio: p. 10; marekuliasz: p. 11 t; mimomy: p. 11 l; NataLima: p. 11 cr; Billion Photos: p. 11 br; Bodor Tivadar: pp. 12, 14 l, 15 tl, 27 t; Arthur Balitskii: p. 13 cr; Morphart Creation: p. 13 b; Neil Lockhart: p. 15 c; Africa Studio: p. 15 b; daseaford: p. 16; mcherevan: p. 17 t; jgorzynik: p. 17 cl; Shi Yali: p. 17 cr; Arcansel: p. 17 b; Underawesternsky: p. 18 b; bioraven: p. 19; GoodStudio: p. 20; Shpak Anton: p. 21 tr; Ron and Joe: p. 21 cl; Anneka: p. 21 cr; NorSob: p. 21 bl; akilasaki: p. 21 br; Luca Ponti: p. 23 t; Siaivo: p. 23 b; Morphart Creation: p. 24 b; Preto Perola: p. 25 bl; Quick-Sale.de: p. 25 br; NataLima: p. 26 tr; MaryMo: p. 27 b; James Steidl: p. 29 t

Library and Archives Canada Cataloguing in Publication

Available at the Library and Archives Canada

Library of Congress Cataloging-in-Publication Data

Available at the Library of Congress

Crabtree Publishing Company

www.crabtreebooks.com   1-800-387-7650

Published in the United States
Crabtree Publishing
347 Fifth Avenue
Suite 1402-145
New York, NY, 10016

Published in Canada
Crabtree Publishing
616 Welland Ave.
St. Catharines, ON
L2M 5V6

Printed in the U.S.A./072022/CG20220201